Proud to be Inuvialuit

Quviahuktunga Inuvialuugama

Fifth House Ltd.
A Fitzhenry & Whiteside Company
195 Allstate Parkway
Markham, Ontario L3R 4T8
1-800-387-9776
www.fifthhousepublishers.ca

Cover and interior design by John Luckhurst
Photography by Tessa Macintosh
Additional photographs and illustrations by: Steffan Widstrand, GNWT Department of Economic Development (Jacob, page 2), Patrick Kane (ice road, page 6), Donna Berngardt (family in traditional caribou-skin clothing, page 11), Autumn Downey (hunting illustrations, pages 12-13, and caribou illustration, page 7), C.W. Mathers, 1905 / NWT Archives N-1979-058-0001 (historic kayakers, page 12-13), B.W. Brown / NWT Archives N-2001-002-3921 (waiting hunters, page 13), and Wayne Lynch (beluga whales, pages 14-15).

Series editorial by Meaghan Craven

The type in this book is set in 10-on-15-point Trebuchet Regular and 10-on-13-point Tekton Oblique.

Fifth House Ltd. acknowledges with thanks the Canada Council for the Arts, and the Ontario Arts Council for their support of our publishing program. We acknowledge the financial support of the Government of Canada through the Book Publishing Industry Development Program (BPIDP) for our publishing activities.

The author would like to thank the NWT Protected Areas Strategy Secretariat, CIBC, WWF-Canada, and Canadian North, for financial assistance in the completion of this book.

Printed in Canada by Friesens on Forest Stewardship Council (FSC) Approved paper

2010 / 1

Library and Archives Canada Cataloguing in Publication

Pokiak, James
Proud to be Inuvialuit = Quviahuktunga Invialuugama / by James Pokiak and Mindy Willett; photographs by Tessa Macintosh.

(Land is our storybook)
Includes some text in Inuvialuktun.
ISBN 978-1-897252-59-8

1. Pokiak, James—Juvenile literature. 2. Pokiak, James—Family—Juvenile literature. 3. Inuvialuit—Hunting—Juvenile literature.
4. White whale hunting—Northwest Territories—Juvenile literature.
5. Traditional ecological knowledge—Northwest Territories—Juvenile literature. 6. Tuktoyaktuk (N.W.T.)—Biography—Juvenile literature.
I. Willett, Mindy, 1968- II. Macintosh, Tessa, 1952- III. Title.
IV. Title: Quviahuktunga Invialuugama. V. Series: Land is our storybook.

E99.E7P58 2010   j971.9'300497120092   C2010-902239-4

Just as whaling skills are passed along from generation to generation, so are sewing skills. The baby belt Rebecca carries her son in was made by her mother-in-law, Agnes Felix. The Inuvialuit learned how to use baby belts from other Aboriginal people to the south. The border used throughout this book is a detail from Rebecca's baby belt.

Acknowledgements

A book like this doesn't happen with just a few people. Mindy and Tessa were particularly honoured to be allowed to go on a beluga whale hunt with James Pokiak and his family. Usually only the beneficiaries of the Inuvialuit Final Agreement are permitted to go on such hunts. The Tuktoyaktuk Hunters and Trappers Committee (HTC) felt that the stories shared were important for educational purposes, so an exception was made, and for that the authors are truly grateful. Mindy and Tessa hope that readers will set down their own cultural perspectives and try to understand that harvesting whales is a traditional way of life for the Inuvialuit.

James thanks his family, including: his wife, Maureen; daughter Rebecca Pokiak, for sharing her first whale hunt with Mindy and Tessa; and her son, Edward; his brother, Boogie, for all his amazing contributions; and especially Belinda and Brianna Lavallee and their parents, Gary and Janice Lavallee. Without Belinda and Brianna the book just wouldn't be as beautiful as it is. Their smiles and interest in learning about their culture are infectious! Thanks also to James's daughter, Myrna Pokiak, and her grade 4 students at Mildred Hall School.

We are truly indebted to the Prince of Wales Northern Heritage Centre (PWNHC), especially Myrna Pokiak, Dot Vanvliet, Charles Arnold, Brenda Hans, Janna van Kessel, and Barb Cameron. The work the PWNHC has completed on Inuvialuit archaeology sites, history, and beluga whales and their relationship with people was instrumental in creating this book.

Others who helped along the way include: Frank Pokiak and Nellie Pokiak of the Department of Fisheries and Oceans; Richard Binder of the Inuvialuit Joint Secretariat; Mark Andrachuk of the University of Guelph; the Siglikmiut Drummers and Dancers; Tessa Dillon and Joe Nasogaluak; Ryan Taylor for his carving talents; John Elanik for posing while delivering water; Laila Voudrach, resource person with HTC; Deseraye Elias, Julia Steen, Ruby Nasagaluak, Kane Raddi, Jaylene Nasagaluak, Samuel Gruben, Brayden Teddy, and Brianna Lavallee for the community clean-up photo; Autumn Downey for the wonderful drawings; the card players, including Ernest Cockney, David Nasogaluak, and Lennie Emaghok; the reviewers, including John Stewart, Gladys Norwegian and Charles Arnold; the translator, David Nasogaluak; Ms. Barb Prevedello and Ms. Sara Spencer along with the grade 4 class at The York School in Toronto; and Tara Neate, teacher librarian, and the grade 3 and 4 students at Joshua Creek P.S., Oakville, ON.

Thanks also to Mindy's husband, Damian Panayi, and their two children, Jack and Rae, for reading early versions and for allowing her the time and space to follow her dreams.

Tessa sends big hugs to her husband, Mike, for being such a great fan and for understanding what the North means to her. And hugs also to Mindy for her incredible energy, which enables Tessa to do her favourite kind of work.

This book is dedicated to my *nanuk* and *dadduk*, Edward and Violet Kikoak, and my parents, Bertram and Lena Pokiak, for raising us children to know who we are.

Proud to be Inuvialuit

Quviahuktunga Inuvialuugama

By JAMES POKIAK
and MINDY WILLETT

Photographs by Tessa Macintosh

FIFTH
HOUSE

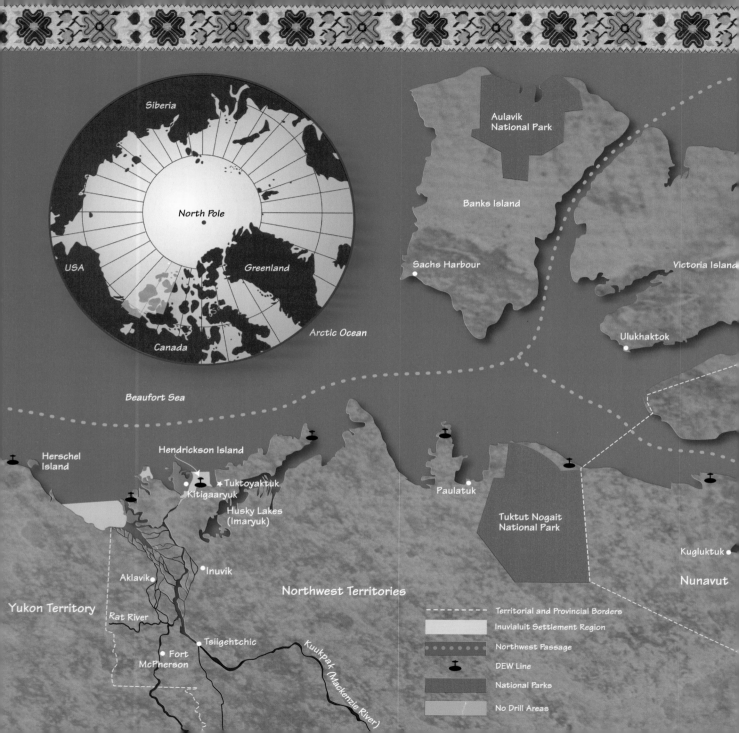

Siberia

North Pole

USA

Greenland

Arctic Ocean

Canada

Aulavik
National Park

Banks Island

Victoria Island

Sachs Harbour

Ulukhaktok

Beaufort Sea

Herschel
Island

Hendrickson Island

Tuktoyaktuk

Kitigaaryuk

Husky Lakes
(Imaryuk)

Paulatuk

Tuktut Nogait
National Park

Kugluktuk

Inuvik

Aklavik

Northwest Territories

Nunavut

Yukon Territory

Rat River

Tsiigehtchic

Kuukpak (Mackenzie River)

Fort
McPherson

- - - - Territorial and Provincial Borders

Inuvialuit Settlement Region

Northwest Passage

DEW Line

National Parks

No Drill Areas

Beluga skin is bumpy and soft.

Aquana,

Uvunga atiga James Pokiak. I am Inuvialuit, which means "real people." Inuvialuit are the most westerly Canadian Inuit. I was born in Sachs Harbour on Banks Island and raised in Tuktoyaktuk, which is on the Arctic coast of the Northwest Territories. I grew up in the old Inuvialuit lifestyle, learning traditional values and survival skills.

This story is about my family, my community, and the importance of keeping our traditions and teaching them to the young in our ever-changing world. Although we harvest fish and caribou like many Aboriginal people in the NWT, our main source of food is the beluga whale. The beluga whale harvest is very important to all of us in maintaining our culture. I know this is hard for some people to understand, but I hope that as you read my story you can see that whale harvesting helps us maintain our culture and that we only harvest what we need. *Quviahuktunga Inuvialuugama*. I am proud to be Inuvialuit.

Quyannanini,

James Pokiak

My Family

I grew up in a large, traditional family with 15 brothers and sisters. By the time I was old enough to hunt my father was losing his sight, so he wasn't able to teach me the ways of the land. Instead, I learned what I know from my older brother, Boogie, my uncle, John Kikoak, and Elder Gordon Anaviak. They are very knowledgeable and I am grateful for all that I learned from them.

My wife, Maureen, and I have 3 children, Myrna, Rebecca, and Jacob. We also have 4 grandchildren. We also spend a lot of time with our friends' children, Brianna and Belinda, and treat them as if they are our own. I'm teaching them what I know so they, too, can be proud to be Inuvialuit.

James's son, Jacob, is learning everything he can from his dad.

James, Maureen, and Belinda share a meal at home.

Myrna is a teacher in Yellowknife. Here she and a student are looking at a museum display she developed about her family and beluga whale hunting.

James and Maureen's daughter, Rebecca, with her son, Edward.

James's brother, Boogie, knows a lot about the land and the history of the Inuvialuit people.

Atuaksavut Qilalukkat Sivuniptingnun
Whales for the Future

3

My family and I are *Tuktuyaktumiut*, people from Tuktoyaktuk. It's a long word, isn't it? Most of us just say we're from "Tuk." Our language is called Siglitun. It is one of the dialects of the Inuit language called Inuvialuktun.

Everybody knows everybody in Tuk! People often gather in the evenings to play cards or music.

About 900 people live in Tuk, which is on the Arctic coast above the Arctic Circle.

Tuk is now a modern community with a school and a pool. In the summertime, Brianna and Belinda can be found playing on the monkey bars under the midnight sun.

Our Words

ulu — *woman's knife*

tuktu — *caribou*

-haq — *material of, or the raw material of*

-muit — *people from that place*

-jaq — *looks like*

-tuuq — *place of many*

-paula — *soot*

Some of our community names are phonetically spelled: Tuktuujaqtuuq, Ulukhaqtuuq, and Paulutuuq. Use the word chart above to figure out what they mean. Then, use the map on page vi to find out how the names are often spelled today.

The answers can be found on page 24.

Our people have a long history of contact with others, including explorers like Sir John Franklin, who tried to find the Northwest Passage. By the late 1800s there were many whaling ships here, and many of my people died from the diseases the sailors brought with them.

A Hudson's Bay Company post was established in Tuk in 1937. Today Tuk is a base for oil and gas exploration in the Beaufort Sea.

All the different people brought new ways of thinking and changed our way of life.

After WWII the Canadian and American governments were worried about Soviet Russia's military strength. They built the Distant Early Warning (DEW) Line across the North. It was designed to warn about a Soviet attack. Tuk became the hub from which supplies were sent to workers on the DEW Line. You can see part of the DEW Line here, behind where they are netting.

Tuk is very much a part of the modern world. We have cell phones and live in modern houses, but we are remote. To get to our town you have to fly, go by boat, or you can drive here on an ice road in the winter.

After the snow melts the community works together to clean up garbage, just as you do in your community.

Tuk has a small pool that is open during the summer. In the winter, people travel 150 km to Inuvik to use the big pool there. They drive on an ice road. Ice roads are built across frozen ground or frozen water each winter in the North.

Homes in Tuk have a tank to hold water. Once or twice a week the water truck comes and fills up the tank. Houses also have sewage tanks that must be pumped out.

Our Stories
How Tuk Got Its Name

Although Tuktuyaktumiut live in the modern world, we try to hold onto our stories, like this one about how Tuk got its name.

As the story goes, there were some caribou that were about to cross to a point of land near where Tuk is today. A young woman was sick, so the people told her, "Don't look out at the caribou, you're sick. Something might happen to the caribou." She agreed, but when the caribou started swimming across to the point she peeked, and the caribou turned into rocks. To this day, you can see the stone caribou when the water is low. That is how Tuktoyaktuk or, "something that looks like a caribou," got its name.

It is very expensive to shop in the grocery store in Tuk as everything has to be flown in. Milk costs $13.89 for 4L!

As you can see, Tuk is a modern community with some differences. Although times have changed, we still depend on the sea for much of our food. When we hunt, we not only get food but also a sense of pride. I feel good when I get fish or beluga whale to feed my family. All of our children grew up on the land, and I feel proud as a parent when I see them hunt to feed their families and others in the community.

James, Maureen, and Belinda caught whitefish and inconnu in nets they set near town.

Belinda is holding the pipsi, or dryfish, James's family made from their catch. Drying fish is one way to preserve it.

We dry fish to preserve it. Another way to keep fish is to freeze it in the Tuk ice house. The ice house is about 10 m underground, dug right into the permafrost. It looks like an outhouse from the outside, but when you climb down there are 3 hallways with 19 rooms. Each hunting or fishing family gets to use one room. This is how we keep frozen what we catch in the summertime.

James and Belinda climb down the ladder into the ice house.

James lowers his catch down into the ice house with a rope and pulley.

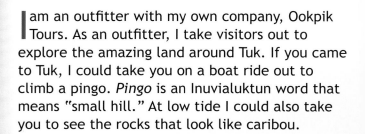

I am an outfitter with my own company, Ookpik Tours. As an outfitter, I take visitors out to explore the amazing land around Tuk. If you came to Tuk, I could take you on a boat ride out to climb a pingo. *Pingo* is an Inuvialuktun word that means "small hill." At low tide I could also take you to see the rocks that look like caribou.

Ookpik Tours gives visitors certificates for enjoying the, "Arctic toe dip" and for crossing the Arctic Circle.

A pingo is a mound of earth-covered ice found only in areas with permafrost. The Tuk peninsula has the highest number of pingos in the world. The largest pingo in Canada, Ibyuk, is here and is at least 1,000 years old. It is almost 50 m high and grows about 2 cm every year.

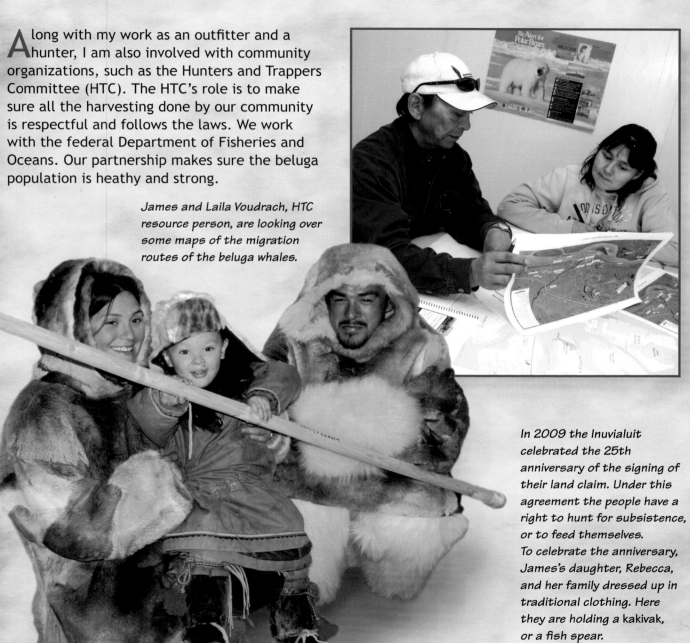

A long with my work as an outfitter and a hunter, I am also involved with community organizations, such as the Hunters and Trappers Committee (HTC). The HTC's role is to make sure all the harvesting done by our community is respectful and follows the laws. We work with the federal Department of Fisheries and Oceans. Our partnership makes sure the beluga population is heathy and strong.

James and Laila Voudrach, HTC resource person, are looking over some maps of the migration routes of the beluga whales.

In 2009 the Inuvialuit celebrated the 25th anniversary of the signing of their land claim. Under this agreement the people have a right to hunt for subsistence, or to feed themselves. To celebrate the anniversary, James's daughter, Rebecca, and her family dressed up in traditional clothing. Here they are holding a kakivak, or a fish spear.

11

A Traditional Qilalukkat Harvest

Tuktuyaktumiut have always harvested whales for subsistence. Harvesting is a community effort because everyone needs to work together to ensure success. We are very thankful that the land and sea have always provided for us.

Inuvialuit hunters, Sydney Ayak and Archie Evigaktuak, looking and waiting for beluga whales, 1956.

Traditionally, Inuvialuit hunted by kayak, which were made from stretched seal skin and driftwood lashed together. The hunter on the right is Bukik, James's great, great grandfather.

1. In July the whales came into an area near Tuk. Many people gathered and worked together to get ready for the harvest.

4. When the whales arrived, the hunters formed a line to circle the whales.

12

The leader told the group of hunters how and where to paddle.

3. Whalers were patient. They waited for the whales to come into view and for the ocean to be calm.

Hunters threw their harpoons, which were attached to a float: an inflated seal skin. Then, they pulled the whales to shore.

6. After the harvest everyone in the community worked together to process the meat and blubber. Traditionally, all the bones and skin were used for tools or skin bags.

Our Stories

The Song that Calmed the Wind

In my language, *uknipkaren* means, "tell me a story." To hunt a whale we must be patient. The ocean needs to be flat calm so that we can see where the whales are gathering. I'm part of the Siglikmiut Drummers and Dancers, and to this day we still tell stories and sing songs of harvesting, like the following song about calm waters.

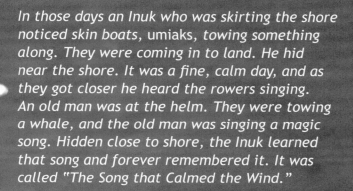

In those days an Inuk who was skirting the shore noticed skin boats, umiaks, *towing something along*. They were coming in to land. He hid near the shore. It was a fine, calm day, and as they got closer he heard the rowers singing. An old man was at the helm. They were towing a whale, and the old man was singing a magic song. Hidden close to shore, the Inuk learned that song and forever remembered it. It was called "The Song that Calmed the Wind."

You that we are towing along
Ah, ya ah e ya
Big whale, big whale,
Stir up the sea with your tail
E ya ah e ya
Give us fair weather today
So we arrive safe and sound on shore.
E ya ah e ya
Tug — tug along hard
E ya ah e ya
Row — Row!

They used another magic call when the whale had been harpooned. When they dragged the sealskin float attached to the harpoon line they sang:

Drag along, drag along the skin bag;
Whale — lose your strength.

Soon the whale would stop, exhausted. The Inuit boats came nearer to the whale. A large and sturdy harpoon would give her the finishing stroke. Then it was, when towing her to land, the ancients in their boats sang the song. Thus did the hunters of whale conjure up fair weather for their return.

Sometimes the calm water we need happens at 3 a.m. In summer the sun is up all night, so the time of night or day doesn't matter. While waiting, we make sure our tools are ready. Like always, we go near Hendrickson Island. Here the waters are shallow, which makes it easier for us to hunt. Our people have been hunting here for as long as anyone can remember. Because the beluga population here is heathy, we feel comfortable harvesting a small number.

How a *Naulak* and *Avataqtak* Work

A harpoon head is called a naulak. *When hunting beluga, it is best to aim the* naulak *at a place on the whale's body that has lots of blubber. This way, the* naulak *will hold tight. Once the* naulak *is in place, the hunter will give it a tug to make sure it's in there. Then the hunter will release the harpoon head from the rest of the harpoon. It happens in seconds. After a whale is harpooned it is shot so it dies quickly. When whales die they sink. But a harpooned whale can be found because the* naulak *is attached to a float, or* avataqtak.

All harvested belugas are sampled to monitor the health of individuals and the population.

James checks the knots on the ropes, sharpens the harpoon head, and makes sure everything is in good working order.

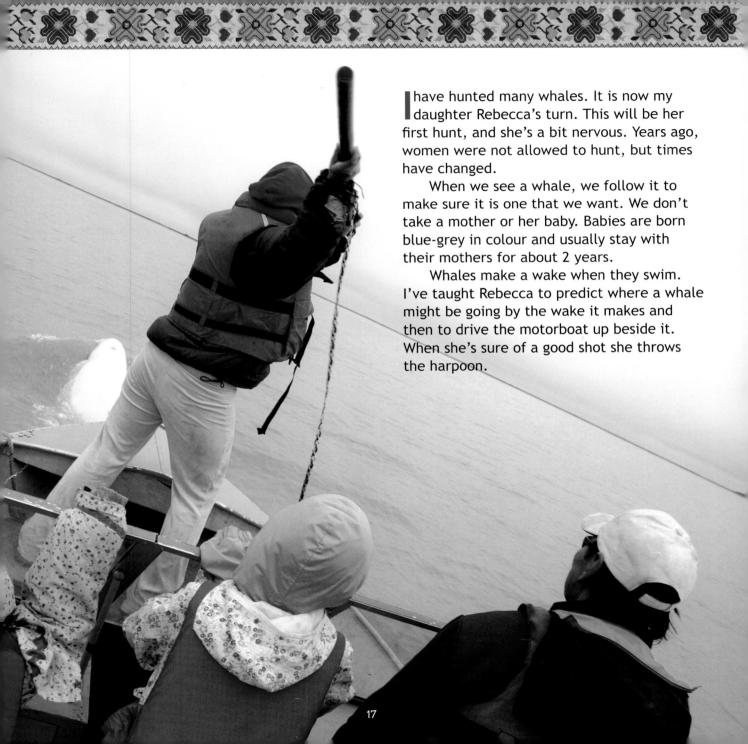

I have hunted many whales. It is now my daughter Rebecca's turn. This will be her first hunt, and she's a bit nervous. Years ago, women were not allowed to hunt, but times have changed.

When we see a whale, we follow it to make sure it is one that we want. We don't take a mother or her baby. Babies are born blue-grey in colour and usually stay with their mothers for about 2 years.

Whales make a wake when they swim. I've taught Rebecca to predict where a whale might be going by the wake it makes and then to drive the motorboat up beside it. When she's sure of a good shot she throws the harpoon.

Once a whale is harpooned and brought in, everyone helps to pull it to shore. At the beach, the real work begins for us. We remove all of the *muktuk* and meat; everything we can use from the carcass. *Muktuk* is the three inner layers of the skin and a layer of blubber.

Hunters attach a rope to the flukes (tail) and pull the whale up to the beach on Hendrickson Island.

The fresh fluke tip is *mamaqtuq* (yummy). It is a traditional delicacy, so we share a little bit of that right away. After all the edible parts are removed from the whale, we take the rest of the body back to the ocean where it will feed other animals.

Nelllie Pokiak using her ulu *to cut up fresh fluke tip to share with Brianna.*

We take all the edible parts home to process. Processing a whale is a lot of work, so the whole family works together.

James made this ulu for his daughter, Myrna. The handle is made from muskox horn.

1. Driftwood is gathered to cook and smoke the whale meat (niqivialuk) and muktuk.

2. Slabs of the muktuk are left out in the sun with the skin side down. When the top, sinewy layer dries, it is easy to cut it off.

3. The muktuk is hung near the fire to drain water and oil. Smoke keeps the flies away and helps to flavour it. An ulu is used to cut muktuk.

4. After a day of smoking, some of the muktuk is boiled, cut into pieces, and stored in the ice house.

James and Maureen cut up boiled muktuk and enjoy it with HP sauce and salt.

5. The niqivialuk is cut into thin slices and hung

6. The thick layer of fat beneath the beluga's skin (uqsuq) is cut up and used to preserve meat. Brianna and Belinda are wearing atikluk to help keep their clothing clean as they work.

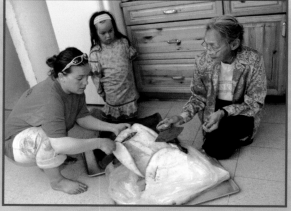

If James and his family harvest 2 whales every year, they will have enough to feed themselves and others, like Rebecca's mother-in-law, Agnes Felix, who lives alone.

Beluga harvests inspire sculptor Ryan Taylor.

While James is drumming, Rebecca, Brianna, and Belinda entertain themselves on the Tuk beach with a traditional game.

Harvesting a whale gives us a real sense of being Inuvialuit. Everyone, of all ages, works together. This is what keeps our culture alive. Traditionally, after a harvest the community celebrates with a drum dance. When I harvest and when I drum it feels good. It makes me feel connected to my ancestors.

I'm proud to be Inuvialuit.

All the Details!

Community Names Challenge from page 5

Tuktuujaqtuuq means "a place of many things that look like caribou."

Ulukhoktuk means "a place where there is lots of material for making ulus [women's knives]."

Paulutuuq is "a place where there is lots of coal."

Tuk Words

Aquana – Hello.

atikluk – an over-shirt, like an apron, worn to protect clothing. The girls wear an *atikluk* when they cut *muktuk*.

blubber – a layer of fat about 10–15 cm thick that insulates belugas from the cold.

dadduk – grandfather.

kakivak – a fish spear that has three sharp points with barbs on each end.

land claim – an agreement between a specific Aboriginal government and the Government of Canada that outlines the rules that each agree to live by. The Inuvialuit signed their land claim in 1984.

mamaqtuq – tastes good.

midnight sun – north of the Arctic Circle (latitude 66 degrees, 33 minutes, or 66°33'N) the sun does not set in the summer. The area is often referred to as "the land of the midnight sun" because the sun is "up" at night. Tuk is at 69°27'N and has 24 hours of daylight from mid-May to mid-July.

nanuk – grandmother.

ookpik – snowy owl.

permafrost – ground that is frozen all year round. The frozen ground may contain ice.

process – taking a hunted animal and cutting it into pieces that can be stored and eaten later.

qilalukkat – more than 1 beluga whale. *Qilalugak* refers to 1 whale.

quviahuktunga Inuvialuugama – proud to be Inuvialuit.

quyannanini - thank you.

Tuktuyaktumiut - people from Tuktoyaktuk.

uknipkaren - tell me a story.

ulu – a knife. From a very early age children are taught to safely use tools, such as ulus.

umiak – skin boat.

uqsuq – the thick layer of fat beneath the beluga's skin. It melts into liquid oil and people use it to preserve meat. It's also like a "chip dip," as Inuvialuit dip their dry caribou, whale, or fish meat into it for flavour.

uvunga atiga – my name is.

Nuligak and Calm Waters

A storyteller, Nuligak, was the first Inuk to publish a book. In this book, he shares a longer version of the story told on page 15 about calm waters. "The Song that Calmed the Wind" is from *I, Nuligak*, by Nuligak, edited and translated by Maurice Métayer, first published 1971, Pocket Books, New York.

About the Inuvialuit

The Inuvialuit (Ee-noo-vee-a'-loo-eet) are closely related to Inuit in other parts of Canada, as well as the Inupiat in Alaska and the Yuit in Siberia. Although related to their neighbours, the Inuvialuit have their own distinct cultural identity, heritage, and dialects.

The Inuvialuit Settlement Region (ISR) was designated in 1984 in the Inuvialuit Final Agreement by the Government of Canada for the Inuvialuit people. It spans 906,430 km² of land and water. The ISR is one of the four Inuit regions of Northern Canada represented by the Inuit Tapiriit Kanatami (ITK), the national Inuit organization in Canada.

Inuvialuktun (Ee-noo-vee-a-look-toon) is one of the 9 official Aboriginal languages of the Northwest Territories. There are three dialects of Inuvialuktun, including Siglitun, which is spoken in Tuktoyaktuk.

The Prince of Wales Northern Heritage Centre is a museum in Yellowknife. It acquires and manages a collection that represents the cultures and history of the Northwest Territories. Visit www.pwnhc.ca to learn more about the Inuvialuit through the online exhibits called: *Inuvialuit Place Names*, *Journey to Kitigaaryuk*, and *An Archaeological Expedition to Kuukpak*. Here, you can listen to the language, learn how to drum dance or make a harpoon, watch videos of harvests, and much more.

Beluga Science

The scientific name for beluga is *Delphinapterus leucas* or "white dolphin without a wing." The population of whales that James harvests is from the Eastern Beaufort Sea stock. The beluga is a toothed whale that eats Arctic cod, herring, and squid. It does not have a dorsal fin. Belugas live in groups called pods. An adult whale will feed James's family for an entire year. If he harvests 2 he has plenty to share with those in need.

Traditional and Scientific Knowledge Working Together

The Fisheries Joint Management Committee (FJMC), the Federal Department of Fisheries and Oceans (DFO), and the Hunters and Trappers Committees (HTC) from Tuktoyaktuk, Paulatuk, Inuvik, and Aklavik work together to manage belugas. For about 30 years they have been watching and learning about the Eastern Beaufort Sea stock, which has a population estimate of about 40,000 whales. Scientists

and harvesters attach satellite-linked tags to some belugas' backs. This allows them to track beluga movements at sea over many months and thousands of kilometres. The population is deemed to be very healthy and the 4 communities only take what they need, which is between 100-130 whales per year. This number is well below what is safe to harvest to maintain a healthy population.

Beluga Facts

Newborn calves	*nalungiatt*	1.5 m	grey
Juveniles (2-5 years)	*tunguvyuit*	2.5 m	lighter colour
Adult females	*nalungialiit*	3.8 m	pure white
Adult males	*anguhalluit*	4.3 m	pure white

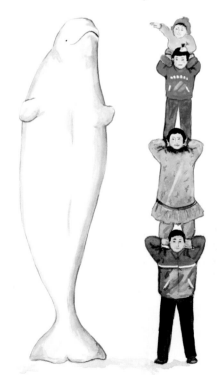

About the Authors and Photographer

James Pokiak is an Inuvialuit subsistence harvester from Tuktoyaktuk, NT. He is an outfitter, hockey player, drummer, and family man. He invites everyone to come on up to Tuk for a visit and to dip their toes in the Arctic Ocean.

Mindy Willett is an educator from Yellowknife, NT. *Proud to be Inuvialuit* is the fifth book she has co-authored in *The Land is Our Storybook* series. Mindy really enjoyed working on this book as it brought her back to the Arctic coast where she was a teacher for 4 years.

Tessa Macintosh is an award-winning Northern photographer who raised her family in Yellowknife. She is grateful for so many memorable experiences at Tuk, from the surprising "un-chill" of dipping her toes in the Arctic Ocean, to the low resonant beat of drum songs.

Brianna and Belinda Lavellee are in grades 4 and 2. They really enjoy school and hardly ever miss a day. Their favourite things to do are: travelling to the cabin with James to hunt and fish, and playing with James's grandsons, Lucas and Edward.